I0108361

Written by: Joanie Boney

Illustrations: Natasha Kostovska

I LOVE MY GLASSES!

Paige, felt her face turn red as she saw and heard her classmates, pointing at her with grins on their faces. Paige, stared at the wall, but she could still hear the taunts from her classmates.

YOU LOOK SILLY!

HEY, FOUR-EYES!

She was the only second grader in her class with glasses, Paige felt alone from the other students. None of the other students had glasses. It was only Paige.

She hated her glasses. She had gotten them over the weekend because her mother and father had taken her to get her eyes checked, and the eye doctor had suggested getting glasses to help her see. At first, Paige loved her glasses. She loved the way she looked in them and she loved how far she could see.

But now, she hated her glasses. Every time she looked in a mirror, she wished she could take her glasses off. Anything to prevent her from wearing them, and anything to keep the other students from teasing and bullying her about them.

Because of her glasses, Paige, was bullied to the point of making her cry. At lunch, she did not sit with her usual group of friends because they teased her too much. She sat at her own table in the lunchroom because no one wanted to share the table with her.

At recess, she played by herself and watched the other kids play in groups, laughing and having fun.

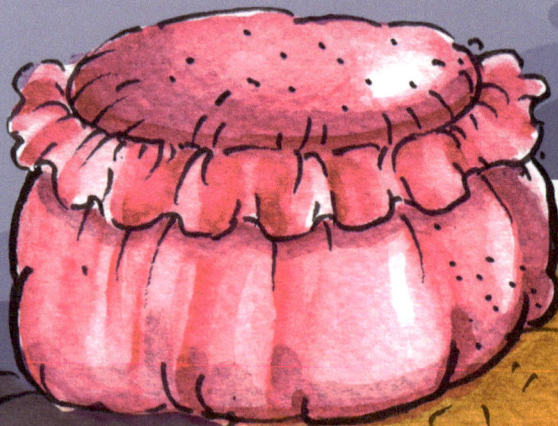

When Paige came home from school that day, she went straight up to her room and buried herself under the covers of her bed. She took off her glasses and placed them on the night table that stood next to her bed.

She hated her glasses. Her mother sat down on the edge of Paige's bed. "Honey, what's wrong?" she asked softly. "You came straight up here after school. What's got you down?"

Paige shrugged and pulled the sheets tighter over her head.

"Come on, Paige," her mom sighed, pulling the sheets back. She pulled her daughter into a sitting position and hugged her close.

"Are the glasses bothering you?"
"Why would you say that?" Paige asked.

"You seem pretty quiet," her mom observed, stroking Paige's hair. "You're usually really happy when you come home from school. You weren't very happy today." Paige shrugged. "It's about the glasses, isn't it?" her mom guessed with a knowing smile.

Paige sighed and hopped off her bed. "Yeah, it's my glasses. All the other kids in my class make fun of me for wearing them and it really hurts my feelings. I like my glasses, but the other kids don't."

Her mom smiled as she led Paige down the kitchen for dinner. As she filled Paige's dinner plate, she said, "It's okay if the other kids don't like your glasses. It only matters if you like your glasses."

"Really?"
Paige asked
as she climbed
into one of the
chairs at the
kitchen table.

"Absolutely," her mom said as she sat down in the chair next to her and rubbed her back softly. "It only matters if you like your glasses. Don't let the other kids in your class determine what you like and don't like."
Paige stared at her.
"Are you sure?"

"I'm absolutely sure," her mother said. "If you like your glasses, that is all that matters. After all, you can see better with them, can't you?"
Paige nodded a little.

The next day at school, Paige walked into her classroom with a large smile on her face. She had matched her outfit to match the color of her glasses, which were pink. She sat down at her table with a smile on her face.

Her mom had given her another pep talk that morning on the way to school to make Paige feel better, and she did feel better. She felt happy about wearing her glasses because she liked being able to see and she loved her pink color frames. She loved everything about her glasses and she was ready to face her bullies.

Paige's confidence was the key to battling her bullies. During breaks in the teacher's lesson plan, a few boys came up to her table and made horrible comments on her glasses, but she simply smiled at them.

They returned to their seats with confused looks on their faces.

Paige practically skipped to the cafeteria. She sat at her usual table in the corner and she was about to unpack her lunch when a few girls came up to her saying "You look weird four eyes". Paige smiled at them.

The girls simply shrugged and left,
a little bewildered with Paige's behavior.

After lunch, Paige went out for recess and a boy in one of the other second grade classes came up to her and sat down in the empty swing next to her.
"I really like your glasses!" he said with a smile.
Paige stopped swinging and looked at him.
"Really? You actually like them?"
"Yeah!" he said.
"I think they look really cool!"
Paige said "I love my glasses too!"
Paige burst into a huge smile that wouldn't leave her face.

COLORING
BOOK

available at:

www.joaneyboneybooks.com

Joanie Boney has always been fascinated by words - poems, letters and short stories. As an author, she has directed her writing to giving young children a sense of belonging, self confidence and a sense of togetherness. Her children's books will introduce readers to a multicultural and multiracial population that she believes reflect the true America.

Joanie is a baby boomer, who loves cats and sitting outside in the summer relaxing in her gazebo, writing while watching her husband feed the birds and those nervous squirrels running around in their back yard. Oh yes and there is that big fat ground hog that eats their organically grown melons every year.

Joanie and her husband of 25 years own U-Impact Publishing LLC. She is a licensed real-estate professional with an extensive background in property management, development and proposal writing.

www.ingramcontent.com/pod-product-compliance
Lightning Source LLC
Chambersburg PA
CBHW041546040426
42447CB00002B/59